DISTRICT 61 DODGE COUNTY

THE WONDERWORLD OF SCIENCE

DISTRICT 61 DODGE COUNTY

By

WARREN KNOX
GEORGE STONE
MORRIS MEISTER
DORIS NOBLE

•

Illustrated by
ALMA FRODERSTROM

Book One

CHARLES SCRIBNER'S SONS · NEW YORK
CHICAGO · BOSTON · ATLANTA · SAN FRANCISCO · DALLAS

ACKNOWLEDGMENT

The authors wish to thank all those who have assisted in the development and trial of the materials used in this series. Experimentation was concerned particularly with pupil interest, grade placement, appropriateness of activities, and reading comprehension. The authors are especially grateful to the following teachers and supervisors who have been generous in their contributions to this textbook project:

MISS LOUISE ADAMS, Teacher in Primary Grades, School 16, Albany, N. Y.

MRS. FAITH LE FORT DUFFY, Teacher in Primary Grades, Edgemont School, Scarsdale, N. Y.

MISS CATHERINE DUTWEILER, Teacher in Primary Grades, East Street School, Hicksville, N. Y.

MISS NELLIE GRIFFITHS, In Charge of Elementary Work, Training School, North Texas State Teachers College, Denton, Texas.

DR. B. B. HARRIS, Dean, North Texas State Teachers College, Denton, Texas.

MISS MOLLY MAE HARRIS, Specialist in Reading, East School, Long Beach, N. Y.

MISS ELEANOR B. MASON, Librarian, Edgemont School, Scarsdale, N. Y.

MRS. HELEN MILLER, Teacher in Primary Grades, Nicholai Street School, Hicksville, N. Y.

MISS AGNES MONAHAN, Teacher in Primary Grades, School 16, Albany, N. Y.

MISS NINA PLANTZ, Principal, East Street School, Hicksville, N. Y.

MISS CARRIE M. SMITH, Cold Spring Harbor, N. Y.

MISS TAMAR WHEATER, Teacher in Primary Grades, Nicholai Street School, Hicksville, N. Y.

MISS EPSIE YOUNG, Teacher in Grade Two, Training School, North Texas State Teachers College, Denton, Texas.

Many thanks are due also to the hundreds of boys and girls who have served as willing and interested helpers during the period of trial and experimentation. The authors hope that children everywhere will be thrilled with their adventures in THE WONDERWORLD OF SCIENCE.

COPYRIGHT, 1940, BY CHARLES SCRIBNER'S SONS

Printed in the United States of America

H

CONTENTS

WHERE PLANTS AND ANIMALS LIVE

Where Animals Live	9
How Animals Move	
What Animals Eat	
Where Plants Live	20
Farm Plants and Animals	22
City Plants and Animals	27

WATER AND LAND

At the Lake	30
On the Hill	34
Land Is Made Up of Rocks and Soil	
The Sand Table	38

THE AIR AROUND US

In the Airplane	43
The Glass of Air	47
Air Takes Up Room	
Wind	51
Wind Is Air That Is Moving	
Rain	53
Air Has Water in It	
The Birthday Candle	56
Air Helps Fire to Burn	

THE SKY ABOVE US

The Sun	61
Heat and Light Come from the Sun	
The Moon	66
Light Comes from the Moon	
The Stars	71
Light Comes from the Stars	
Star Pictures	74

THE WORLD IN SPRING

Signs of Spring	81
Days Get Longer in the Spring	
Spring at the Lake	85
Plants in Spring	89
Trees Begin to Grow in the Spring	
Animals in Spring	92
Growing Plants from Seeds	96
Seeds Sprout and Grow in the Spring	

WHERE WE GET OUR FOOD

Making a Garden	103
Food Animals	108
Food Plants	112
Different Parts of Plants Are Used for Food	
Some Foods Are Better Than Others	

WHERE PLANTS AND ANIMALS LIVE

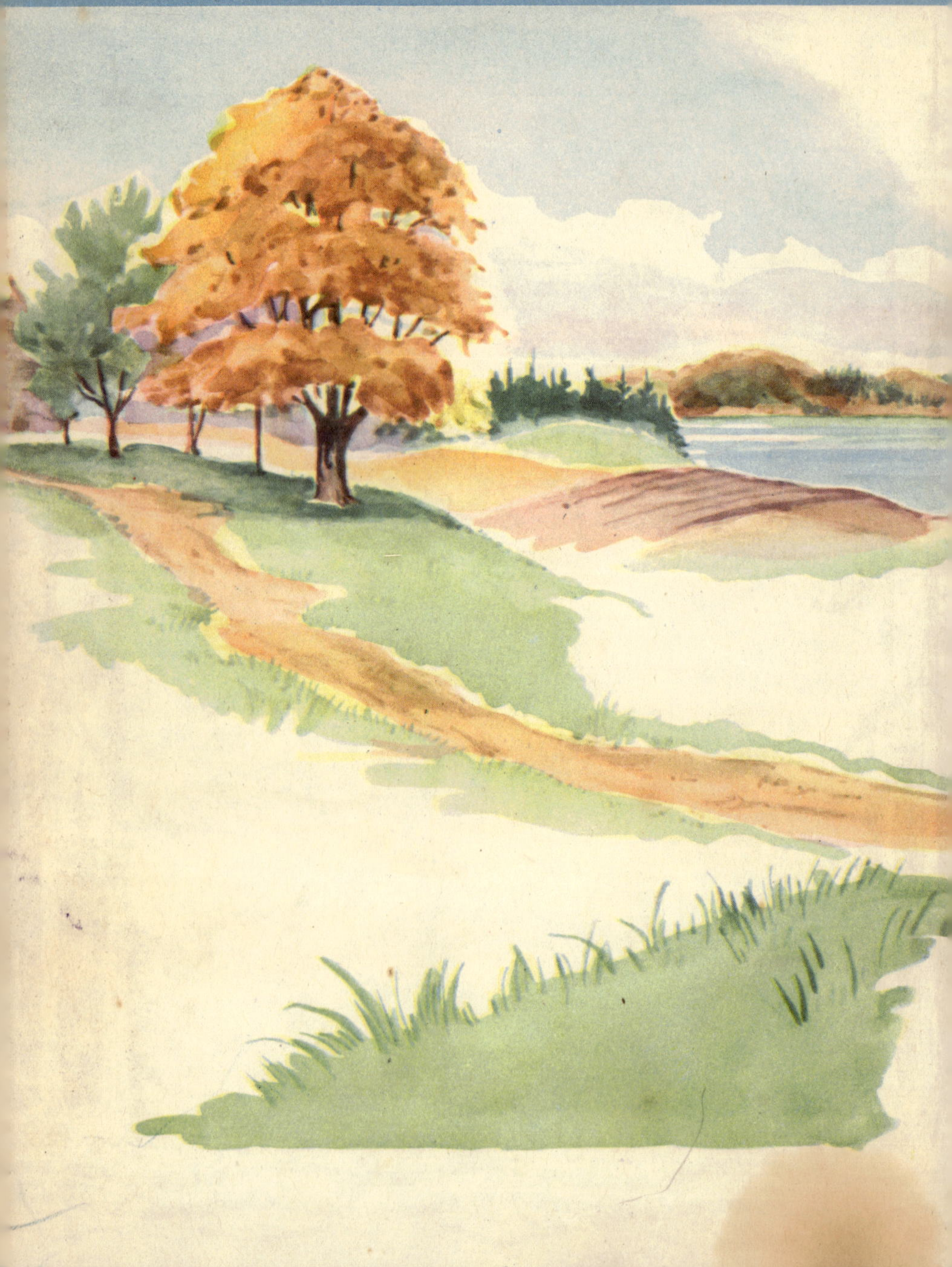

Jimmy and Rex

Here are Jimmy and Rex.

Jimmy and Rex live near a woods.

Where Animals Live

Many plants and animals live in the woods.

Jimmy and Rex like to go to the woods. They like to see the plants and animals.

Here are some animals that live in the woods.

Rex runs after animals.

The animals run to their homes and hide.

Some animals live in the ground.
Some animals live on the ground.
Some animals live in water.
Some animals live in trees.

Some animals eat plants.
Some animals eat other animals.

Animals You Know
What animal is this?
What does he eat?
Where does he live?

Do you know this animal?
What does he eat?
Where does he live?
How does he move?

What animal is this?
What color is he?
Where does he live?
How does he move?

What animal is this?
What color is he?
Where does he live?
How does he move?
What does he like to eat?
What animals run after him?
Where does he hide?

Where Plants Live

Here are some plants.
Some plants live in the ground.
Some plants live in water.
Trees are big plants.

Do You Know?

1. What animals does Rex run after?
2. Is Rex an animal?
3. Do animals move?
4. How do animals move?
5. Where do plants live?
6. Do plants live near your home?

Name an Animal

1. Name an animal that lives in the woods.
2. Name an animal that lives in the ground.
3. Name an animal that lives in the water.
4. Name an animal that lives in trees.
5. Name an animal that lives near your home.

Farm Plants and Animals

Jimmy and Alice like to go to the farm.

Many plants and animals live on the farm.

Here are some animals that Jimmy and Alice saw on the farm.
How many do you know?

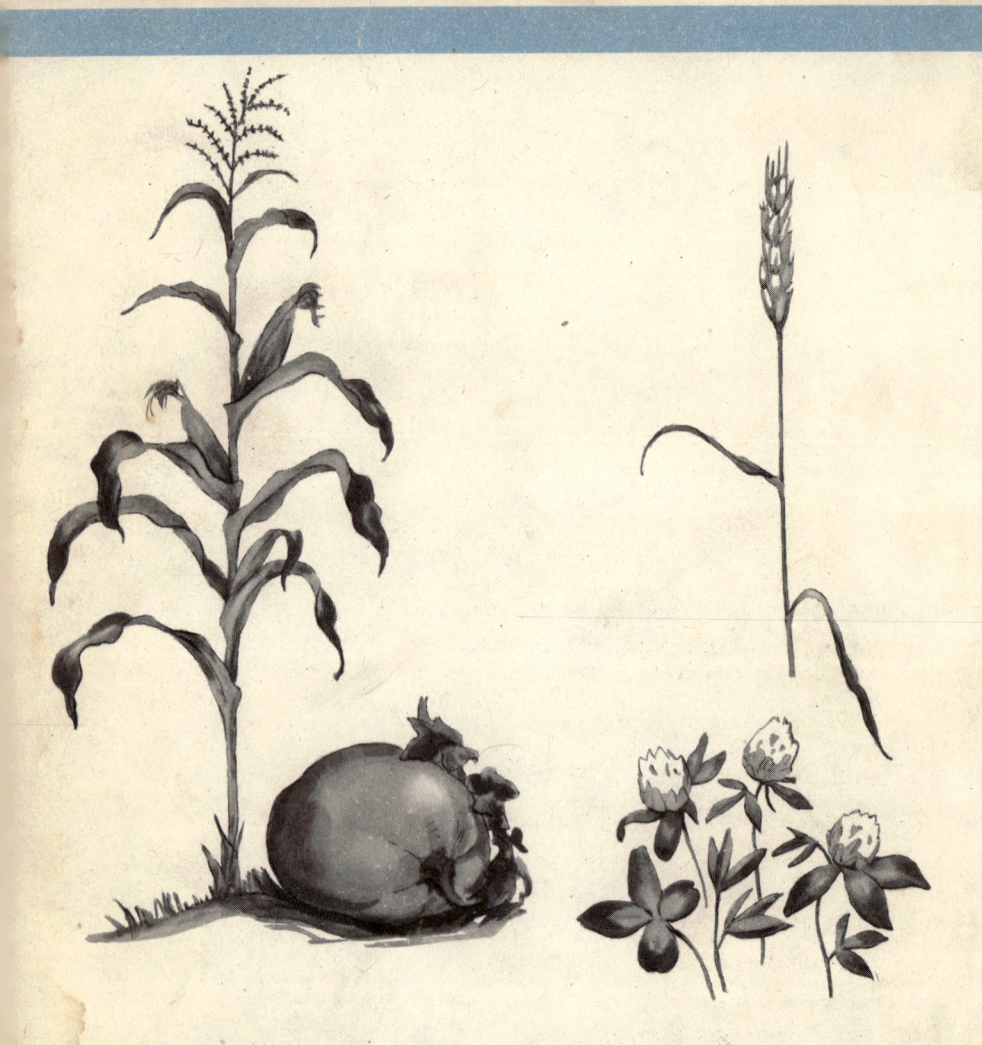

Here are some plants that Jimmy and Alice saw at the farm.

How many of them do you know?

Can you bring some of them to school?

Alice said, "I want to make a farm. Let us make a farm in school."

Alice said, "I see some animals. Animals live in the city, too."

City Plants and Animals

One day Jimmy and Alice went to the city.

Jimmy said, "I see some plants that live in the city. I do not see many animals in the city."

Here are some plants that live in school.

Jimmy gives them water.

Do some plants live in your home?

WATER AND LAND

At the Lake

Jimmy's father has a boat. The boat is on a lake.

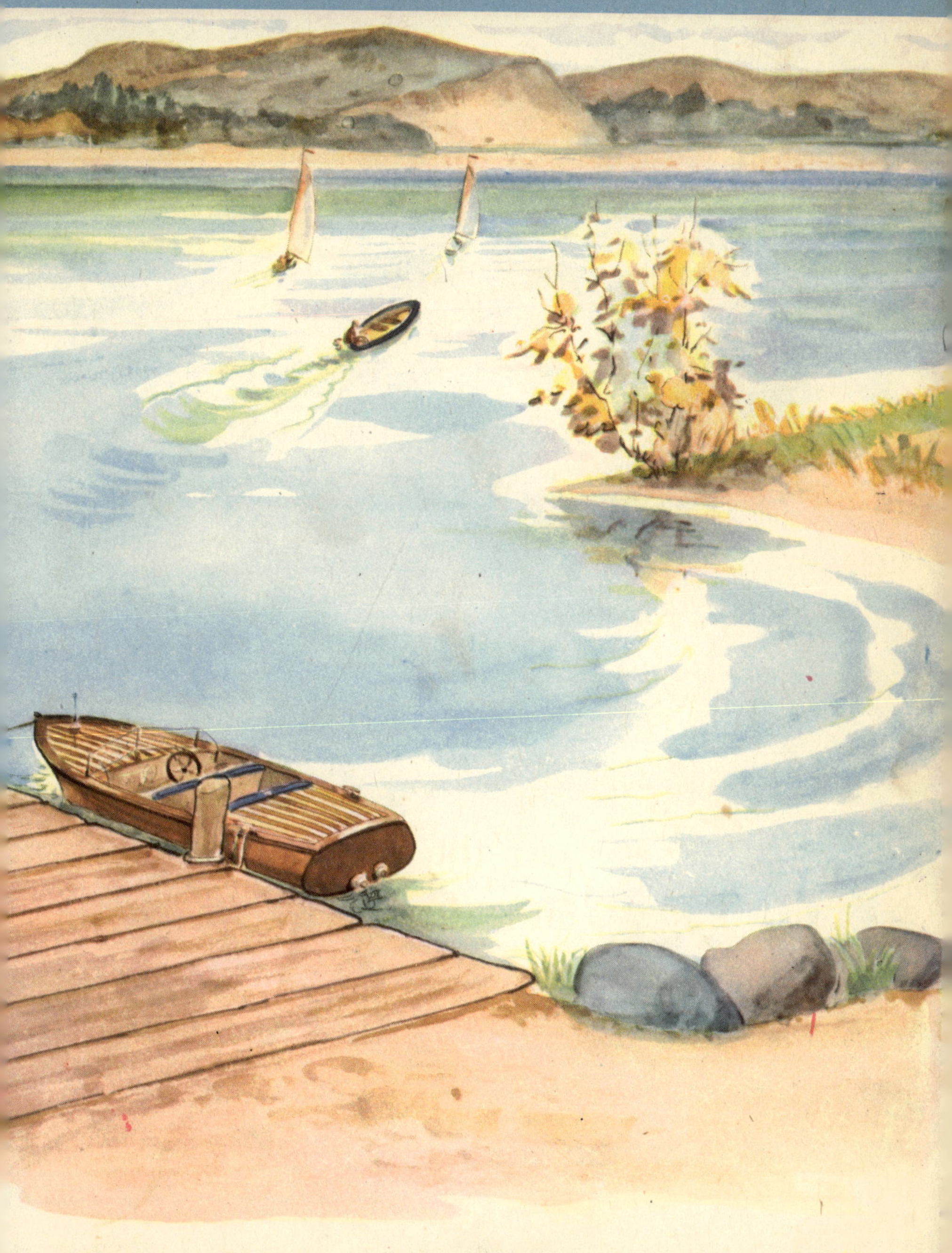

One day Jimmy, Alice and Father went to the lake. They went for a ride in the boat.

There was a big hill near the lake. After the boat ride Alice said, "Let us go up the hill."

On the Hill

The hill was made of rocks and soil.
There were big rocks and little rocks.
Many plants and animals lived on the hill.

They went to the top of the hill.
They saw water and land.
The lake was water.
The other hills were land.

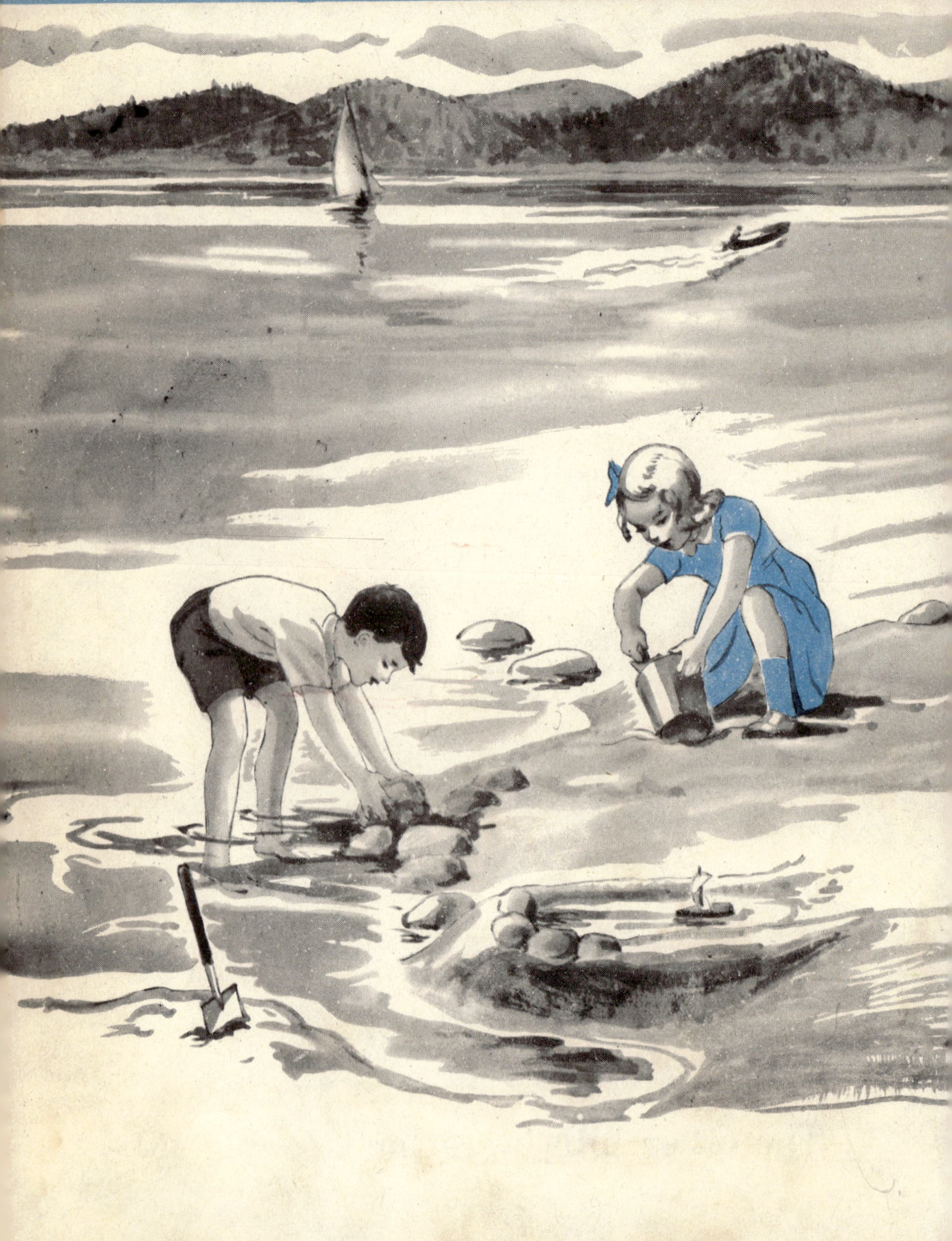

They went down the hill to the lake.

"Let us play in the sand," said Jimmy. "I like to play in the sand."

"We can take some sand home with us," said Alice. "Then we can play in the sand at home."

The Sand Table

At home Father made a sand table.

"Let us put land and water in the sand table," said Alice.

Jimmy put soil and rocks in the sand table.

He made hills with the soil and rocks.

Alice made the lake.

She put sand near the lake.

Jimmy made some boats.
He put the boats on the lake.
Alice made houses.
She put the houses on the land.

Do You Know?

1. Where did Jimmy go?
2. Where did Alice go?
3. Where did Father go?
4. What did they see from the lake?
5. What is a lake?
6. What are hills made of?
7. Are rocks living things?
8. What is sand?
9. What did Jimmy make?
10. What did Alice make?

Things to Do

1. Make some boats.
2. Put water and land on a sand table.
3. Put boats on the water.
4. Make hills in the land.
5. Put plants on the hills.

THE AIR AROUND US

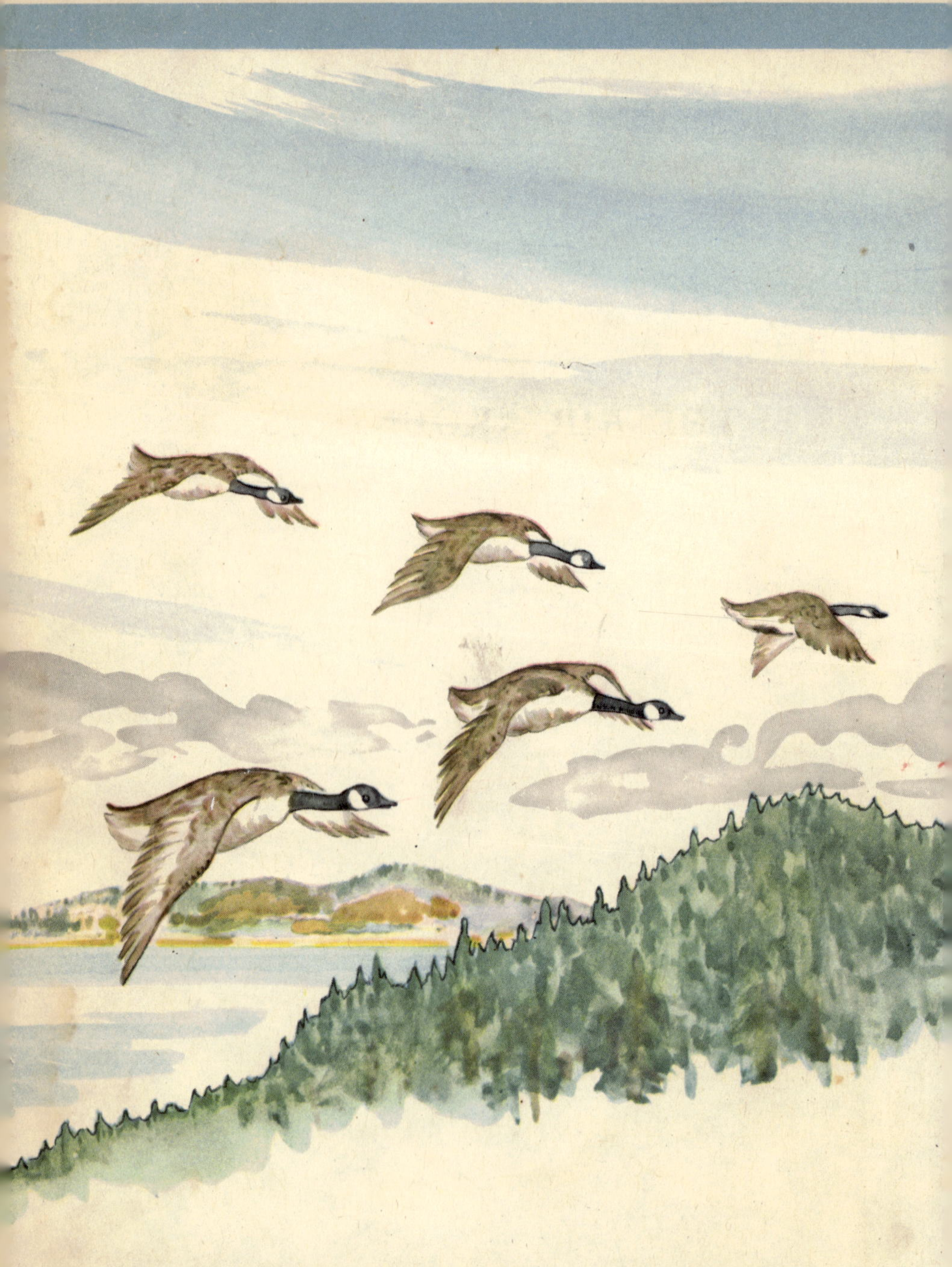

In the Airplane

One day Jimmy and Alice went up in an airplane. Father went with them.

The airplane went high up in the air.

"Look at the ground," said Father.

Jimmy and Alice saw houses and trees. They saw water and land. They saw a lake.

The things they saw looked little. It was fun to go up in the airplane.

The airplane went higher and higher. Alice looked down. She saw the clouds.

"Jimmy," she said. "Do you see where we are? We are higher than the clouds."

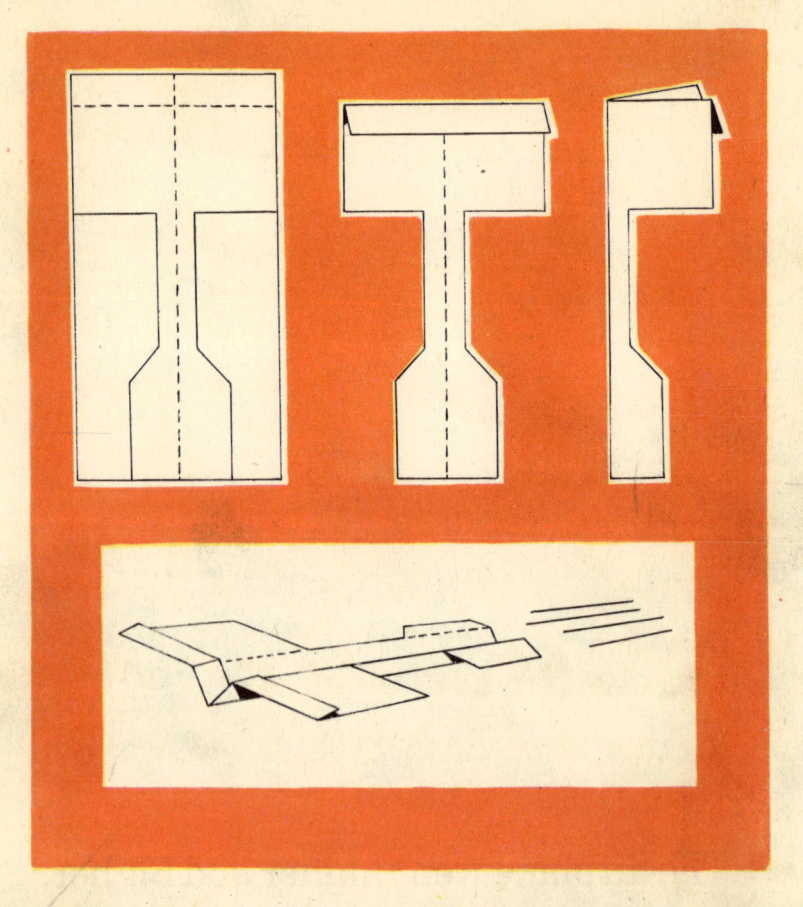

Jimmy made this airplane. He made the airplane out of paper.

Can you make an airplane?

Can you make it go up in the air?

The Glass of Air

Jimmy has a glass. Is there anything in the glass? What do you see in the glass?

There is a glass on the table, too.

Is there anything in the glass on the table?

What do you see in this glass?

Now Jimmy holds the glass under water.

Does the water go in the glass? Try to find out.

Jimmy put some soil in the glass.
He put water on the soil.

Did anything come out of the soil?
Do as Jimmy did and find out.

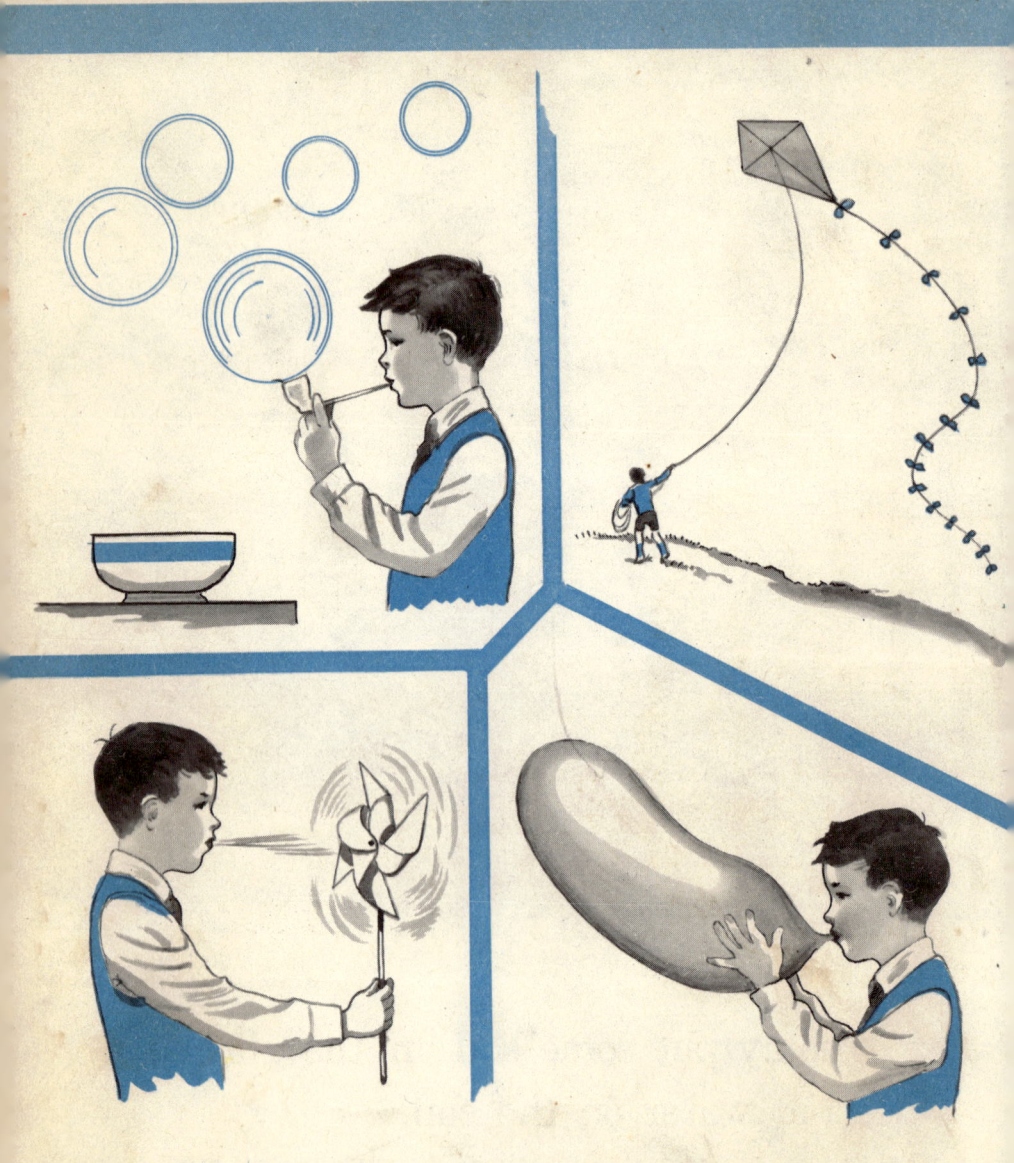

Here are some things you can do.
What did you find out about air?

Wind

Alice is making the air move.
Do you know what moving air is?

Jimmy and Alice are going home from school. The wind is blowing.

The wind pushes against Jimmy and Alice. It pushes against the houses and trees.

Moving air is wind.

Alice said, "It is going to rain. There are dark clouds in the sky.

"The big, dark clouds have water in them. Let us run home."

The rain came before they got home.
Rex came to meet them.

Jimmy said, "I like the rain."
Rex does not like rain.

The Birthday Candle

It was Alice's birthday. She had a big cake. There were six candles on the cake.

Do you know why the cake had six candles?

When they were eating the cake, Jimmy said, "I am going to try something. I am going to put my candle under a glass."

Jimmy put the candle under the glass. Then the light went out. It was dark in the room.

Does the candle need air to burn?

Do You Know?

1. Can you see air?
2. What is wind?
3. What did Jimmy and Alice find out about air?
4. What comes from clouds?
5. What did Jimmy and Alice see from the airplane?
6. What color are rain clouds?
7. Why were there six candles on Alice's birthday cake?

Yes—No

1. A candle will burn without air.
2. Rain comes from clouds.
3. Wind is air that is moving.
4. Clouds have water in them.
5. Air is all around us.

THE SKY ABOVE US

60

The Sun

One sunny day Jimmy and Alice were looking at the sky.

"Do you know why it is day time?" asked Jimmy.

"Yes," said Alice. "The sun makes it day time. The sun shines on the earth and makes it light."

"The sun must be very big," said Jimmy.

"Yes," said Alice. "The sun is very big and very hot.

"Father told me about the sun. He said that it is bigger than the whole earth. There is no water or land on the sun. There are no plants or animals.

"The sun is burning hot. It is very far away."

"But the sun is not very hot today, is it?" asked Jimmy. "It is a cold day.

"There are ice and snow on the ground. There is ice on the lake. There is snow on the house and on the trees."

"Do you want to find out if the sunlight is warm?" asked Alice.

"Hold this glass in the sunlight. Then hold your hand near the glass."

"You are right," said Jimmy. "The sunlight is hot. It is too hot to hold my hand near the glass."

"I am going to try something," said Jimmy. "I am going to hold the glass near some paper."

When Jimmy did this, the paper burned. Jimmy found out that sunlight is hot.

The Moon

The moon is round like the sun. It is not as far away as the sun. It is not as big as the sun.

Sometimes we see the moon at night. Sometimes we see the moon in the day time.

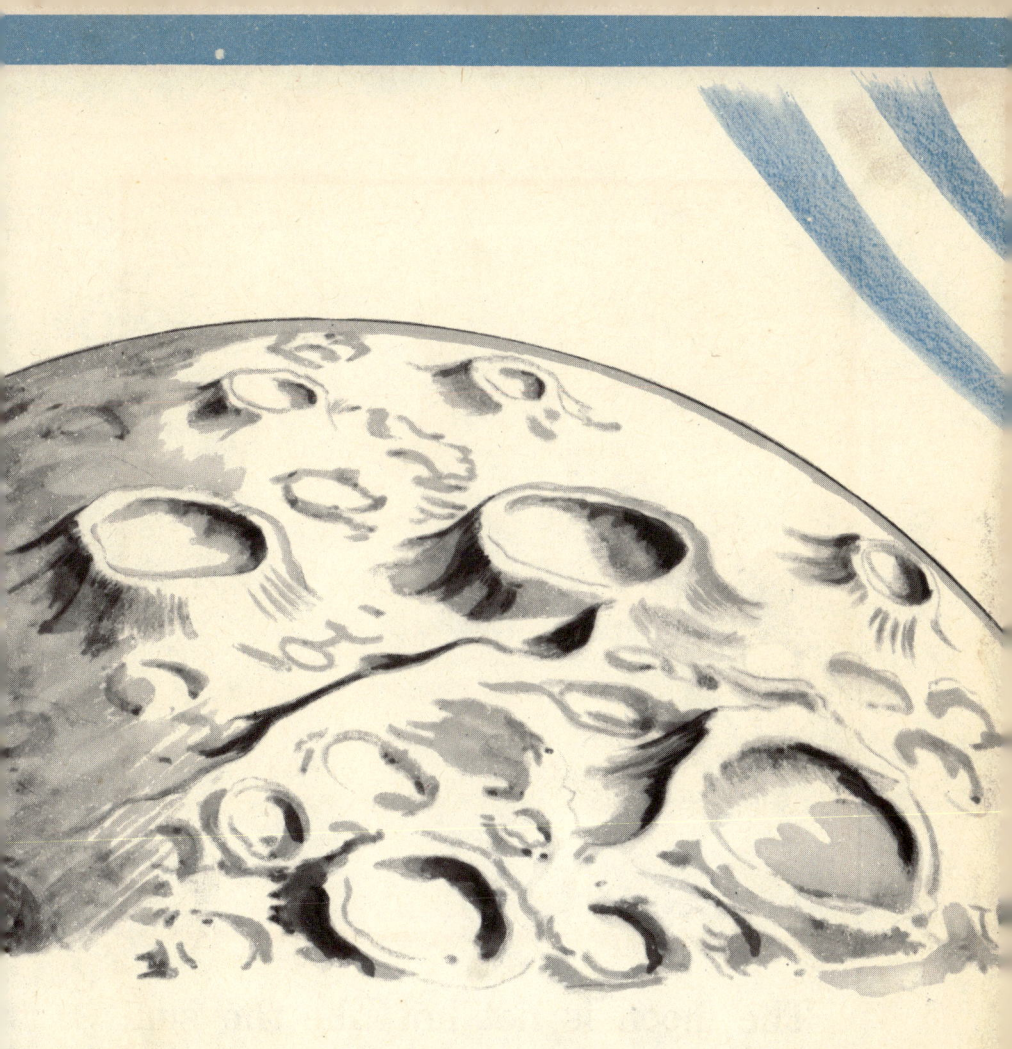

No one could live on the moon. There is no water or air on the moon.
There are no clouds on the moon. There are no plants or animals.

The moon is not hot like the sun.
The moon gets all of its light from the sun.
When we look at the moon, we can see the sunlight shining on the moon.

Jimmy has a light. Alice has a ball.
The light is like the sun. The ball is like the moon.

Do you see how the sun lights up the moon?

The moon is always round. But it does not always look round to us.

The light part of the moon is where the sun shines.

The dark part of the moon is where the sun does not shine.

The Stars

At night we can see many stars in the sky.

Do you know what stars are?

Stars are like our sun. They are big and very hot. They are very far away.

The stars are round like the sun and moon.

Some of the stars are bigger than the sun. All of them are bigger than the moon.

Stars look little to us. That is because they are very far away.

We see the stars only at night. But the stars shine in the day time, too.

We can not see the stars in the day time because the sun gives too much light.

Do you know how many stars there are? Do you think you could count them?

Some nights we can not see the stars. That is because there are too many clouds in the sky.

When there are too many clouds in the sky, the light from the stars can not get through. Then the sky looks very dark.

But the stars are always shining. They give light all the time.

Star Pictures

Some stars make pictures in the sky.

Here is one of the pictures that the stars make. The picture looks like a big dipper.

Have you seen the Big Dipper in the sky?

NORTH STAR

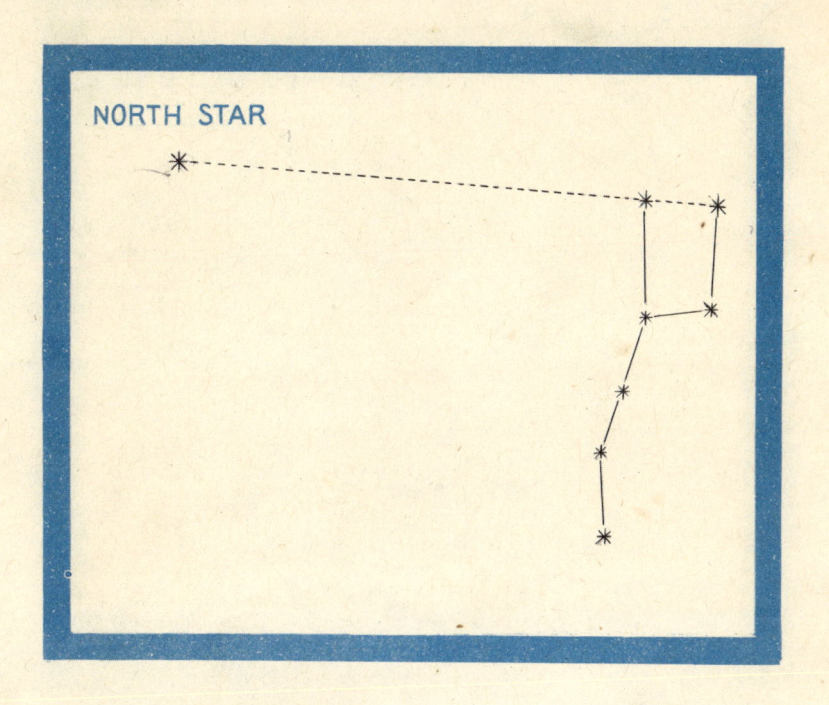

The Big Dipper is in the north. Two stars of the Big Dipper point to the North Star.

The North Star is big but it does not look big to us. It is very far away.

Try to find the North Star in the sky. This star is always in the north.

NORTH

WEST   EAST

SOUTH

When you look north, your right hand is to the east.

Your left hand is to the west.

Your back is to the south.

Can you tell north, west, east, and south?

Things to Do

1. Find out what time the sun comes up.
2. Find out what time the sun goes down.
3. Look at the sky and find a big star.
4. Find the Big Dipper in the sky.
5. Find other star pictures in the sky.
6. Make a picture of the Big Dipper on paper.
7. Make a picture of the sun.
8. Make a picture of the moon.
9. Find north, east, south, and west in the school room.
10. Find out if your house is north, east, south, or west of the school.
11. Find north, east, south, and west at home.

Do You Know?

1. What are stars?
2. Could you live on the moon? Why?
3. Could you live on the sun? Why?
4. Can we always see the sun? Why?
5. Can we always see the stars? Why?
6. How does the sun give light?
7. How does the moon give light?
8. Why do the stars look little to us?
9. Can you count all the stars?
10. How can you find the North Star?

Yes—No

1. Big animals live on the moon.
2. The sun is a big star.
3. The moon is bigger than the sun.
4. Stars are round.
5. There are trees on the moon.

THE WORLD IN SPRING

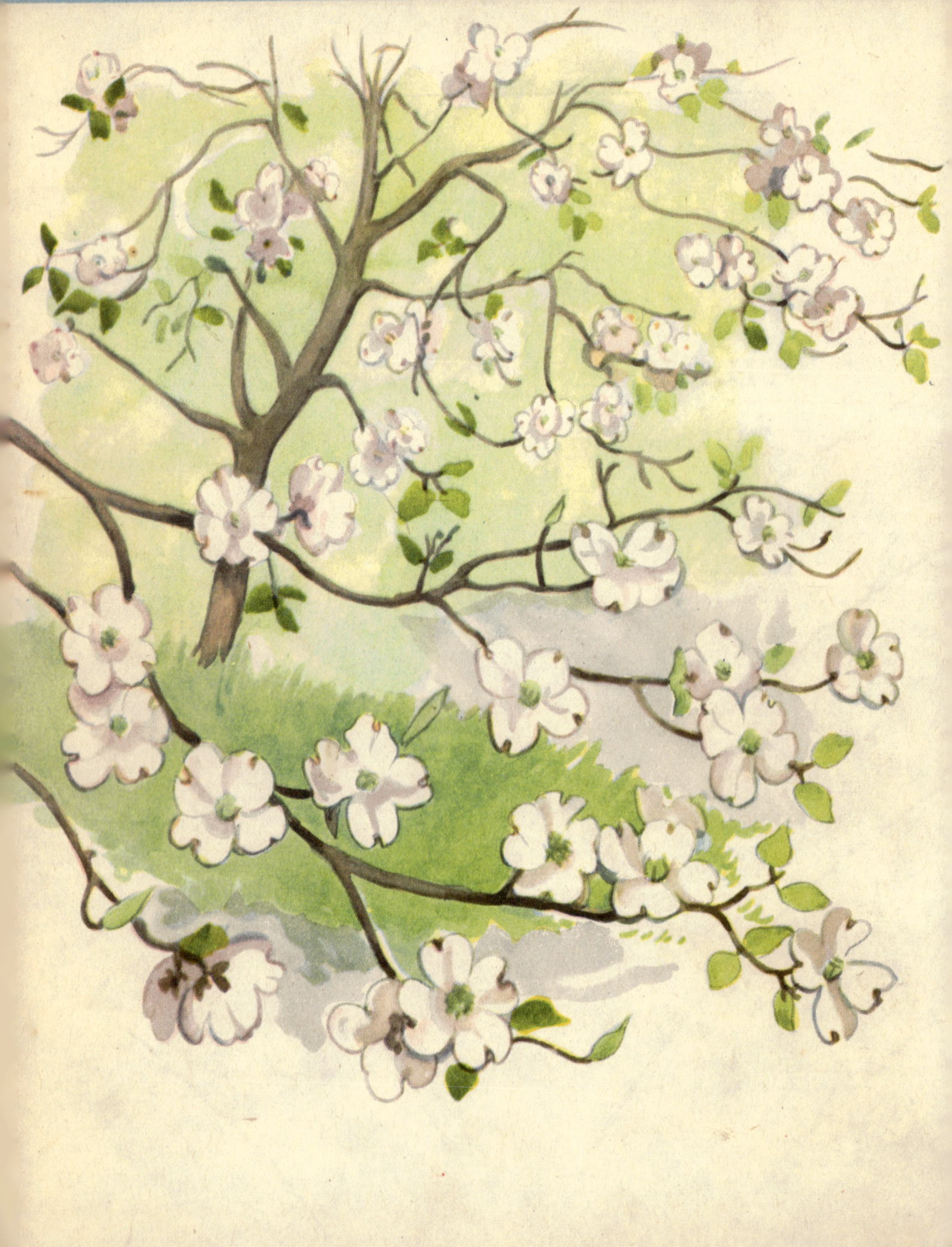

Signs of Spring

"Do you see what I see?" said Alice to Jimmy.

"Here is a flower that has come up through the ground. It is a very pretty flower. Now I know that it is spring."

"Do you know why it gets warm in spring?" asked Alice.

"I know one thing that makes spring warmer than winter," said Jimmy. "The days are getting longer. We get more light and heat from the sun."

"I know something that makes it warmer, too," said Alice.

"Do you see where the sun is? It is higher up in the sky.

"When the sun gets higher up in the sky, the earth gets warmer. That makes the flowers grow up through the ground."

In the winter the sun is not very high up in the sky. It does not make the air and soil very warm.

In the spring the sun gets higher up in the sky. It makes the air and soil warmer.

Spring at the Lake

"I would like to go to the lake," said Jimmy.

"In winter there was ice on the lake. It was fun to go on the ice. Do you think there is ice on the lake now?"

"Let us go and see," said Alice.

Jimmy and Alice are on their way to the lake. They are going through the woods. They see some signs of spring in the woods.

What signs of spring do you see in this picture?

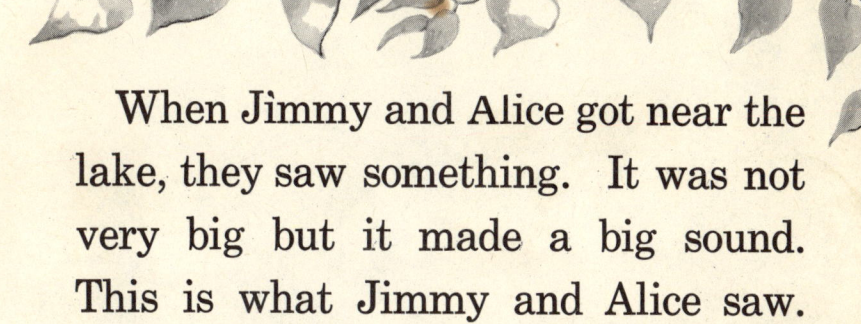

When Jimmy and Alice got near the lake, they saw something. It was not very big but it made a big sound. This is what Jimmy and Alice saw.

Did you see any of these animals this spring?

Do you know what kind of sound they make?

Jimmy and Alice are at the lake. "Oh!" said Alice, "there is no ice on the lake at all. Where did the ice go?"

"I know," said Jimmy, "the ice has been changed to water. The heat from the sun changes the ice to water."

Plants in Spring

"Here is something that has changed, too," said Alice.

"See how big the buds are on this tree. In winter the buds were little. Why are the buds big now?"

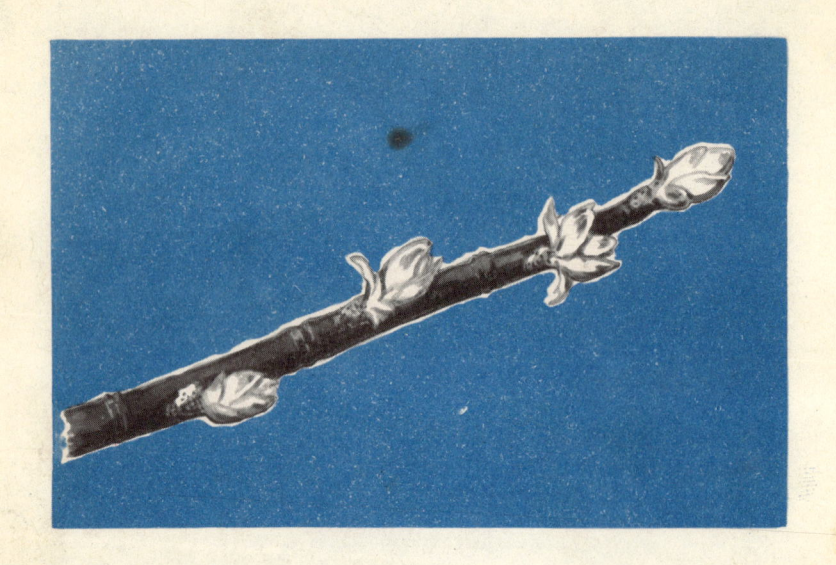

"Let us find out," said Jimmy. "Let us open some of the buds."

In some of the buds there were little leaves. In other buds there were flowers.

"I know why the buds get bigger in spring," said Alice. "It is because the leaves and flowers in them are growing."

Jimmy and Alice looked around the lake. They saw many more signs of spring. They saw plants with pretty colors. They saw many animals, too. What plants and animals did Jimmy and Alice see around the lake?

Animals in Spring

On the lake there were some ducks. The ducks were swimming in the water.

"These ducks were not here in the winter," said Alice.

"No," said Jimmy. "Ducks like to swim in the water.

"In the winter the lake was covered with ice. The ducks could not swim in the ice."

"Why do ducks like to swim in the water?" asked Alice.

"That is because they get their food from the water," said Jimmy.

"Ducks eat fish. They eat plants that grow in the water, too."

"Oh, look," said Alice. "There are some more ducks."

Many ducks were coming to the lake. They made a pretty picture flying through the air.

Here are the birds that Jimmy and Alice saw in the woods.
Do you know all of them?
What colors are they?
Did you see any of them this spring?

Here are some other animals that we see in spring.

Do you know what animals they are?

These animals sleep all winter.

They sleep in dark places under the ground.

Growing Plants from Seeds

Jimmy and Alice are planting some seeds in a box. They put the seeds in soil. They put water on the soil. Then they put the box in the window.

What do you think will happen to the seeds?

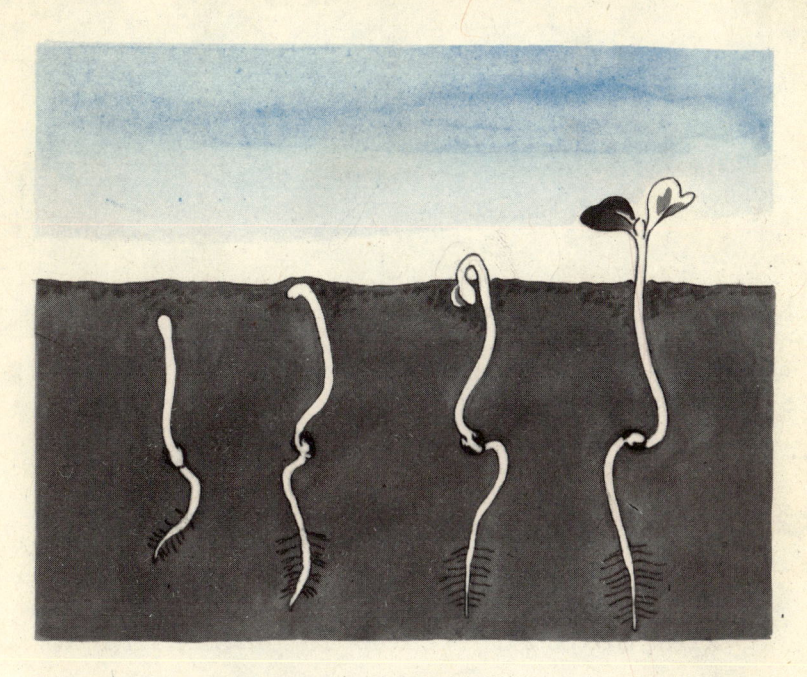

One side of the box was made of glass. Jimmy and Alice could see through the glass. This is what they saw.

Roots came out of the seeds. The roots went down in the soil. Then the stems came out of the seeds.

The stems went up to get air and light.

The sunlight came in the window. Jimmy put water on the soil every day. Soon the little plants came up above the ground.

The little plants got bigger and bigger. The soil gave them water. The sun gave them light.

It was fun to see the plants grow bigger.

Things to Do

Look for signs of spring.

Plant some seeds in a box of soil.

Look for birds that come from the south.

Make a picture of a duck swimming in the water.

Make a picture of a duck on land.

Go to a lake and look for plants and animals.

Find out more about animals that wake up in spring.

Make a picture of a spring flower.

Look for plants that are coming out of the ground.

Find the little leaves in the buds.

Look for leaves that are coming out of the buds.

Do You Know?

1. Why is spring warmer than winter?
2. What are in the little buds on trees?
3. What do the plants get from the soil?
4. What happened to the ice on the lake?
5. What are some of the signs of spring?
6. What are some animals we see in spring?
7. What are the parts of a plant?
8. Are ducks plants?
9. What do ducks eat?
10. What are some birds you saw this spring?

WHERE WE GET OUR FOOD

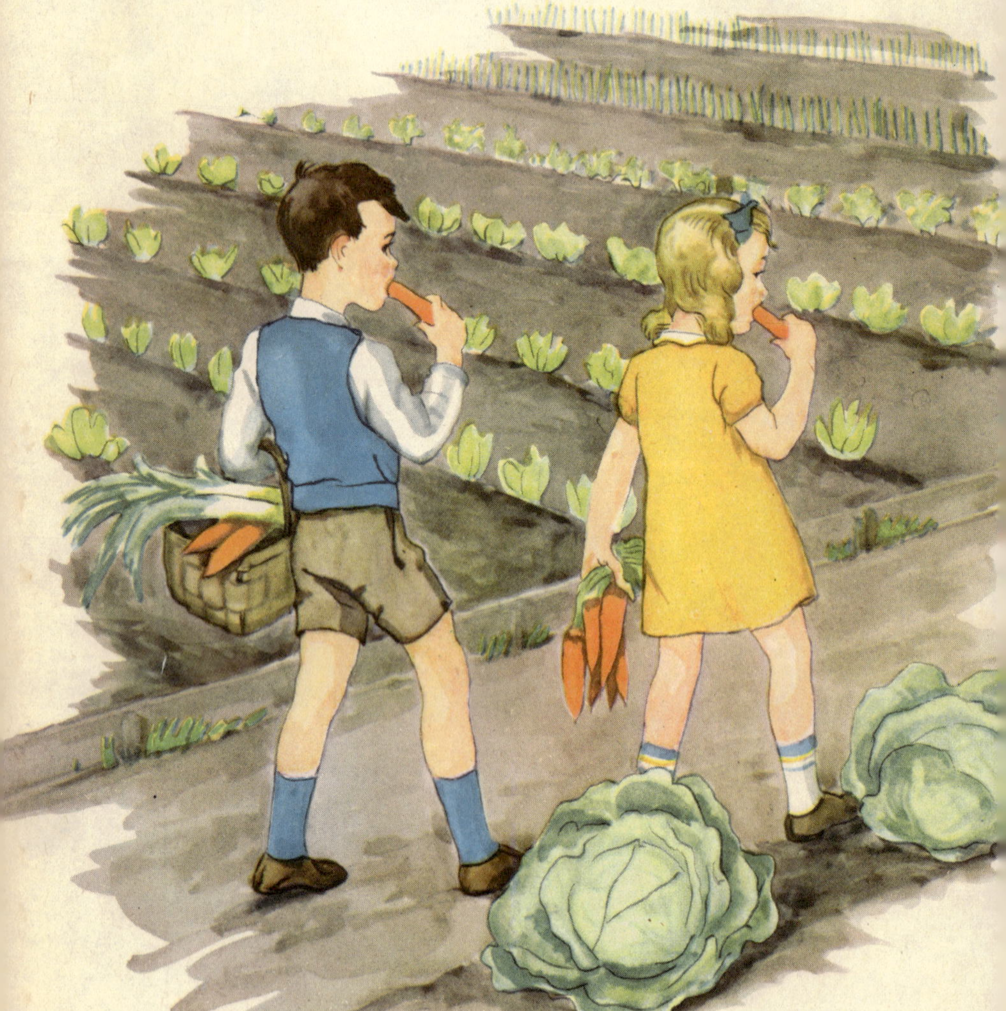

Making a Garden

"Oh, how I like to eat," said Jimmy.

"It is fun to eat. I think I could eat all the time."

"I like to eat, too," said Alice. "But I could not eat all the time. Too much food is not good for us."

"Vegetables are good for us," said Jimmy.

"I know something that would be fun," said Alice. "It would be fun to make a garden."

"Oh, yes," said Jimmy. "Then we can grow some vegetables."

"We can get some ground back of the house. We can dig it up so that the plants can grow. Then we can plant the seeds."

"That will be fun," said Alice.

"I will help you make the garden. We can plant some seeds right away.

"We have some vegetable plants in the box at school. Let us plant them in the garden, too."

Look at the garden that Jimmy and Alice made. They have big plants and little plants in the garden.

Some plants came from the box in the window at school. Some plants came from seeds.

Jimmy and Alice dig in the garden every day.

One day Jimmy and Alice were in the garden.

"Look," said Jimmy, "some of our plants are growing big. I think we can eat them now."

"Let us take some of them in the house," said Alice. "We will have them for dinner."

Here are some of the other foods that Jimmy and Alice eat for dinner.

These foods did not grow in the garden. Some of them came from plants. Some of them came from animals.

The foods on the right came from plants.

The foods on the left came from animals.

Food Animals

Here are some animals that give us food.

What animals are they?

What foods do we get from them?

Cows live on the farm. They like to eat grass.

Cows give us milk. Milk is a very good food for us.

Many other foods are made from milk. One of them is ice cream.

Here are some other animals that give us food.

What animals are they?

What foods do we get from them?

Jimmy and Alice are using up food. They need food to keep them moving.

All of us need food to keep us moving. We need food to keep us warm. We need food to make us grow.

We need to eat many kinds of food. We need food that comes from plants. We need food that comes from animals.

← LEAVES

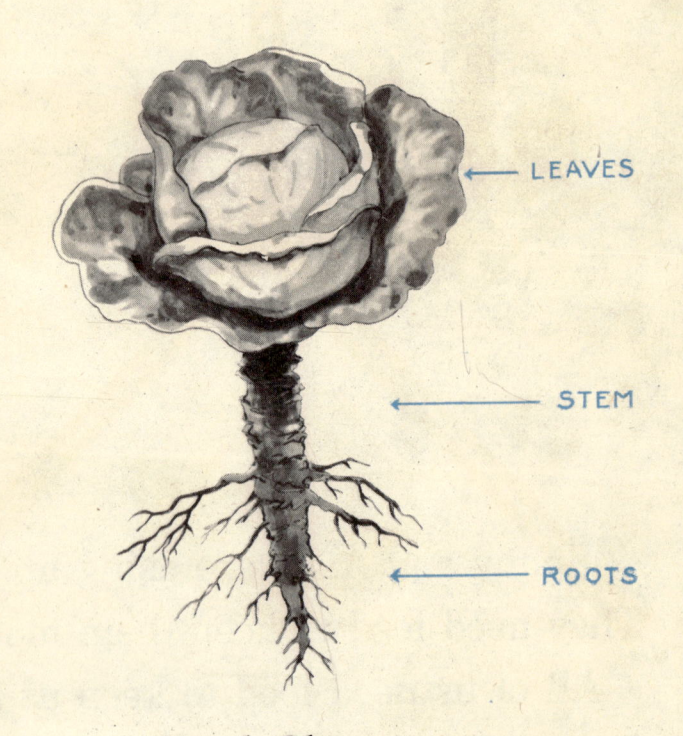

← STEM

← ROOTS

Food Plants

We eat the leaves of some plants. We eat the stems of some plants. We eat the roots of some plants.

The plants that give us food have leaves, stems, and roots.

We eat the leaves of these plants.

The leaves of these plants are very good for us. They help to make us grow.

We should eat some green plants every day.

We eat the stems of this plant. Stems are between the leaves and the roots.
Some stems are good to eat. Some are not good to eat.

We eat the roots of these plants. Their roots are big and round.

Roots grow in the soil. They have much food in them. They help to make us grow and keep us warm.

Some of the fruits that Jimmy and Alice like to eat grow on these trees. Do you know what kind of trees they are?

Here are some other plants that give us food.

Do we eat the roots, stems, or fruits of these plants?

Many of our foods come from the seeds of plants.

What foods do you see in this picture?

From what kinds of seeds do these foods come?

We eat some foods that have seeds in them. But we do not eat the seeds. These foods are fruits.

Most fruits grow on trees. Some fruits grow on trees near where you live. Some fruits grow far away.

Some fruits are round and some are long. Some have pretty colors.

We should eat some fruit every day. It is very good for us.

Do You Know?

1. What did Jimmy and Alice have for dinner?
2. What are some foods that come from animals?
3. What are some foods that come from plants?
4. What parts of plants do we eat?
5. What are some foods that are very good for us?

Which is Right?

1. Milk comes from   plants   animals
2. Plants grow from   seeds   animals
3. Roots grow in the   air   ground
4. Fruits grow on   trees   animals
5. Leaves of plants grow in the   air   ground

NOTES

The world of science and nature is a new world of adventure for children. Wonder, or child curiosity, given encouragement and direction, leads to all the thrills that accompany real learning of the truths of science. The authors believe that truth is fascinating and properly emotional in its appeal to young adventurers in science. These books are written in the language of children and with the most careful regard for accuracy of content. The authors believe also that learning in science should be an integral part of an elementary school program which is designed to help children live happily in their social and physical worlds. The material included in these science books was carefully planned with respect to childhood interests and needs and arranged in accordance with the seasons so as to promote real learning through the use of a wealth of available materials and appropriate activities.

The activities and experiences described and suggested are arranged in a natural learning sequence as determined by careful trial in a large number of typical urban and rural elementary school classrooms. The science materials are organized in a flexible learning-unit form which facilitates adaptation to local programs of study and permits their use as the motivating cores or important parts of larger projects in an integrated elementary school curriculum. The content was carefully checked with curriculum materials proposed in various State Syllabuses and in such reports as the 31st Yearbook of the National Society for the Study of Education. The rich and comprehensive content represents the contribution of research in elementary school science and of a long experience with a nature study program in American elementary schools.

In the construction of these books, major attention has been given to the reading problem. Child language and simplicity of vocabulary dominate the style of the reading material. The illustrations were carefully planned along with the text and present a most worthwhile series of science learning experiences. The manuscript was carefully checked by experienced classroom teachers and by reading experts, line by line and page by page. The vocabulary was checked against such standard word lists as the Thorndike, the Gates and the Stone. These books may be used as basal texts in science or as reading material in connection with an integrated course in reading. They are planned so that reading may be a means to an end and so that children may be able to center their interests in the science subject matter and satisfy their natural curiosity concerning the world in which they live.

Where Plants and Animals Live, pp. 5-28

Jimmy and Alice discover that plants and animals live in the ground, on the ground, in water and in trees. They observe plants and animals in the city and in the country. What can a teacher do to help her children make this discovery? Plan simple excursions: to the park, to the woods, to a museum; display many pictures.

Pages 6–7. This illustration introduces a story which children will be able to follow even though they may be unable to read. However, since the text is very simple, most children will learn to read it with very little help. Rex is a police dog.

8. Jimmy's house is in the suburbs of a city. A blue aster is shown in the foreground. Let the children enjoy the picture; then lead them to discuss it freely.

9. Objects shown in illustrations throughout the book will be referred to beginning at the upper left-hand corner and proceeding toward the right around the illustration. Following this order a crow, a squirrel, a quail, and a dragonfly are shown on this page.

10. Sumac, woodbine, fox grapes.

11. Blue jay, red-headed woodpecker, box turtle, porcupine.

12–13. Children will like to tell of similar experiences with animals. Encourage them to talk freely.

14. Above: deer, blue jay, perch. Below: chipmunk. Be sure that children see the relation of illustrations to text.

15. Kingfisher with perch, chipmunk, frog. The frog and the kingfisher eat animals; the chipmunk eats plants.

18. Green frog and cowslip.

19. This is a review page. The rabbit is eating clover. Other questions can be devised and answered by referring to previous text and illustrations.

20. Spruce, cattails, water lilies. Be sure that children see the relation of illustrations to text.

21. Answers to "Do You Know" are: (1) Rabbits and squirrels. (2) Yes. (3) Yes. (4) Walking, running, jumping, flying, crawling. (5) In water; in the ground. (6) Yes, no matter where you live.

Answers to "Name an Animal" according to text are: (1) Deer. (2) Chipmunk. (3) Perch. (4) Squirrel. (5) Rabbit. Many other correct answers are possible also.

22. Farm, ducks, rooster, hen, sow and pigs.

23. Horses, cows, sheep, chicks.

24. Corn, wheat, clover, pumpkin.

25. Children will usually want to carry out this activity themselves.

26–27. This sketch was made in Central Park, New York City.

28. Jimmy watering geraniums and begonias.

Water and Land, pp. 29-40

The general objective of this section is to aid children in getting acquainted with their physical surroundings. The text suggests numerous activities and experiences which will contribute toward the realization of this objective.

30–31. Children will like to tell of their own travel experiences.

32–33. Jimmy, Alice, and Father are returning from a ride around the lake.

34. Blue jay, birch, bluebird, oriole, ferns.

35. Perhaps there is a place near the school which will be convenient and interesting to explore.

36. Wet sand in a sand table has as great possibilities for construction as it has on the beach.

37. A mullein plant is shown in the border.

38–39. The sand table should be checked to see that it is waterproof before beginning this activity.

40. (1–3) Jimmy, Alice and Father all went to the lake. (4) They saw water and land. (5) A lake is a large body of water surrounded by land. (6) Hills are made of rocks and soil. (7) No. (8) Sand is composed of fine particles of rocks. (9) Jimmy made some boats. (10) Alice made houses.

The Air Around Us, pp. 41-58

The concept of air is often confused with the concept of space by young children. For this reason, experiments which demonstrate the reality of air make good approaches to its study. Blowing through a straw with one end of the straw held under water often convinces a child that air is real. Another interesting experiment is to put some crushed paper in a bottle and invert the bottle in water. The paper remains dry.

42–43. Wild geese. Compare with airplane.

44. Discuss the reason why the houses, the lake, and the trees look small.

45. Notice the shadow of the plane on the clouds.

46. Steps in making a model airplane from a sheet of stiff paper are illustrated. Fold and cut the paper as indicated.

47. The glass Jimmy holds is filled with air.

48. No water enters the glass because the glass is filled with air and the air cannot escape. To show this more clearly, place a cork on the surface of the water before inverting the glass.

49. Bubbles of air come out of the soil as the water takes the place of the air in the soil. Repeat the experiment, using sand and other materials.

50. Pinwheels may be cut from paper and attached to the eraser of a pencil by means of a pin. The pressure of air keeps bubbles and balloons inflated.

51. The definition of wind follows on page 52.

52–53. Children will like to tell of their experiences with wind.

56. Jimmy is testing the hypothesis that fire needs air to burn.

58. Answers to "Do You Know" are: (1) Air cannot be seen. (2) Wind is moving air. (3) (There are numerous answers.) (4) Rain, snow, hail, etc. (5) Houses, trees, water, land. (6) Dark. (7) Alice is six years old.

"Yes-No" answers: (1) No. (2) Yes. (3) Yes. (4) Yes. (5) Yes.

The Sky Above Us, pp. 59-78

The sun, moon and stars are as much a part of our surroundings as are water, air, and animals. The fact that all heavenly bodies are far away seems only to increase children's interest in them.

62. Even large buildings look small in the distance.

63. On a cold day the air, not the sun, is cold.

65. An opportunity for emphasizing safety is obvious.

66. Many children have never observed the moon in the daytime. Point out to them the time of the month to look for it.

67. This illustration is taken from an actual photograph.

68. In this position only half the moon is visible.

69. Compare with illustration on page 68. Perform this experiment in a darkened room. Observe moon from different angles.

70. Beginning at the upper left-hand corner and reading from left to right in each row, the monthly cycle of moon phases is shown.

74–75. The Dipper is shown in winter position.

76. For most children this exercise will require considerable practice.

78. Answers to "Do You Know" are: (1) Stars are suns. (2) No, because it is too cold. (3) No, because it is too hot. (4) No; sometimes the sun is on the other side of the earth, or clouds obscure its light. (5) Sometimes there are clouds in the sky at night. (6) All intensely hot bodies give off light. (7) The moon reflects the sunlight to the earth. (8) Stars are very far away. (9) Counts of the visible stars have been made, but this is not easy to do. (10) A line extended through the last two stars of the Dipper runs in the direction of the North Star.

"Yes-No" answers: (1) No. (2) Yes. (3) No. (4) Yes. (5) No.

The World in Spring, pp. 79-100

Spring is the time when living things are most alive. At no other season are there such great opportunities for observation and understanding of our natural surroundings. Encourage the children's awareness by planning many field excursions. Let them keep a "Diary of Spring" as a class project. In it they may record, with dates and time and place observed, each sign of spring in the neighborhood.

80–81. Dogwood and crocus.

84. It is probably unwise, at this age level, to attempt a more complete explanation of the reason why it becomes warm in spring.

86. Flicker, bluebird, skunk cabbage, frog.

87. Top: birch leaves; below: leopard frog.

88. Willow and pussy willow.

89. Bluebirds on horse chestnut tree.

90. Horse chestnut twig. Secure one and examine carefully. Notice the scars of last year's leaves. Open some of the buds.

91. Crow, garter snake, moccasin flower.

92–93. Mallard ducks, bulrush on page 92, sedge on page 93.

94. Oriole, flicker, brown thrush on nest.

95. Bear, raccoon, chipmunk, woodchuck.

97. Stages in the growth of radish seedlings.

100. Answers: (1) The sun gets higher in the sky. It makes the air warmer. (2) Leaves. (3) Water and minerals. (4) The ice changed to water. (5) Opening of buds, etc. (6) Varies with locality. (7) Roots, stems, leaves. (8) Ducks are animals. (9) Ducks eat a variety of both plant and animal foods.

Where We Get Our Food, pp. 101-120

The primary need of living things is food. Information about food is of great importance to health.

105. String beans, cabbage, lettuce.

107. Left column: eggs, cheese, milk; right column: cake, bread, chocolate.

108. Pig, sheep, turkey, steer.

110. Goat, goose, bee on flower, mackerel.

113. Spinach, lettuce, cabbage.

114. Compare celery with the cabbage on page 112.

115. Beet, rutabaga, radish, carrot.

116. Banana tree, dwarf orange tree.

117. Watermelon, Hubbard squash, string beans, tomato.

118. Left: wheat, corn, oats; right: bread, muffins, oatmeal.

119. Peach, cherries, plums.

120. Answers to "Do You Know" are: (1) See pages 106 and 107. (2) See pages 108–110. (3) See pages 112–119. (4) Roots, stems, leaves, buds, flowers. (5) Milk, vegetables, etc.

"Which is right?": (1) Animals. (2) Seeds. (3) Ground. (4) Trees. (5) Air.

WORD LIST

The total number of words used in this book is 258. Eighty-eight per cent of these words were used at least five times. All words were checked carefully against the Gates, Thorndike and Stone word lists. Of the 258 words, 202 are in the First 500 Words and 40 are in the Second 500 of Gates: A READING VOCABULARY FOR THE PRIMARY GRADES (Revised and Enlarged). The remaining 16 words are either proper names or words explained in the text.

5	12	19	27
where	run(s)	him	one
plant(s)	after	20	day
and	13	big	went
animal(s)	their	21	not
live	home(s)	an	any
6	hide	your	28
—	14	name	give(s)
7	ground	22	29
Jimmy	on	farm	land
Rex	water	Alice	30
here	tree(s)	23	lake
are	15	saw	father
8	eat	24	has
near	other	at	boat
a	16	of	31
woods	you	them	—
9	know	can	32
many	what	bring	for
in	is	school	ride
the	this	25	33
10	does	said	was
like	he	want	hill
to	17	make	up
go	do	let	34
they	how	us	made
see	move	26	rock(s)
11	18	I	were
some	color	city	little
that		too	

35	46	55	62
top	out	—	must
36	paper	56	be
—	47	birthday	very
37	glass	had	hot
down	anything	cake	told
play	there	six	me
sand	48	candle(s)	whole
we	now	why	no
with	hold(s)	when	or
38	under	something	far
table	try		away
put	find	57	63
she	49	light	but
39	come	room	today
house(s)	as	need	cold
40	50	burn	ice
did	about	58	snow
from	51	will	64
living	wind	without	if
thing(s)	52	all	warm
41	blowing	59	sunlight
air	push(es)	above	hand
around	against	60	right
42	53	—	65
—	rain	61	found
43	dark	sunny	66
airplane	sky	time	moon
high	have	asked	round
44	54	yes	67
look	came	sun	could
it	before	shine(s)	68
fun	got	earth	gets
45	meet		69
cloud(s)			ball
than			

127

70	81	93	105
always	flower	food	—
part	pretty	fish	106
71	82	flying	dinner
stars	longer	94	107
our	more	bird(s)	—
72	heat	95	108
because	83	sleep	—
only	grow	place(s)	109
much	84	96	cow(s)
think	winter	seed(s)	grass
count	85	box	milk
73	would	window	cream
through	86	97	110
74	way	root(s)	—
picture(s)	sign(s)	stem(s)	111
Dipper	87	98	using
75	sound	every	112
North	these	soon	—
two	kind	gave	113
point	88	99	green
76	oh	wake	114
east	change(d) (s)	100	between
left	89	—	115
west	bud(s)	102	keep
back	90	—	116
south	open	103	fruits
77	leaves	good	117
—	91	vegetables	—
78	—	104	118
—	92	garden	—
79	ducks	dig	119
world	swimming	so	—
spring	covered	help	120
80			—
—			